Can We Anything We See

Catherine Bresner

SPUYTEN DUYVIL
New York City

Praise for *Can We Anything We See*

"Catherine Bresner's keyword unlocking a speculative ekphrasis, or doing to "cloud" what a prompted AI does to a human hand, messing it uncannily, making strange in its interpretive drift. The blanks above the poet's extracts open the Possible even as they bracket what's happened, captured broken links to an Internet that was so different only yesterday, remember? And if not: recall as these motile and unnerved lines do. While you're there, recall, also, that the cues one writes to MidJourney may set us to picturing, too. Can't you see it? Can't you see anything? *Can We Anything We See*? Bresner, compellingly unsettled, asks. Yes, they/she do."

—Douglas Kearny, author of *Sho*

"In the histories of our halting, weirdly haphazard journeys with AI yet to be written, let's be sure to make space for Catherine Bresner's swift, beautiful meditation on image, caption, technology, self, other. Us and our computers: a strange dialogic space, equally apt to offer ludicrous and/or stunning possibility and the spectacle of our own mortal bodies—still fumbling. The book starts as a series of captions to absent images. Some quite funny. But there's an attention to language, its resilience, and the resilience of the human sensorium that I find bracingly moral. Not that we are offered proscriptions. Instead, Bresner elegantly, conscientiously pries open a dialectical inquiry, where the computational "can" confronts a sensitized "we". It may just be us and our phones, but we are yet making poetry together: "Fertile, blooming / a thousand shapes of us es." This is gorgeously inventive and important work."

—Hannah Brooks-Motl, author of *Earth* and *M*

"Catherine Bresner's *Can We Anything We See* initiates a reverse ekphrasis, as the title's verbal omission is an intentional invitation in this fill in the blank text as collection of captions, many of which mime the encoded prompt-speech of text to image generators, where the only limit of vision or visibility is one's imagination. Some pages read as aphorisms, some as advisories, some as divinations, though all of Bresner's poems explode the "could-scape" of networked intimacies rejiggered through neural networks and the spectacle of always-on copresence: "not solitude exactly but/something like it." Bresner's *Can We Anything We See* is as its amorphous speaker-user intones: a "hallucinatory artifact" beyond the "capitalist gory holes" of our daily scrolls. What we find at the edge is not just the vertiginous horror of unchecked sight, but a site of possible subjectivity: "outside the I space.""

—Chris Campanioni, author of *VHS* and *The Internet is for Real*

"I'd like computers to be able to record everything you think and see. To be like the brain, and to write that out."
>—Bernadette Mayer in conversation with
>Isaac (formerly Lisa) Jarnot, *Poetry Project Newsletter*,
>[Feb/March, 1998]

"Each image fits into place, with the calm of not having too many, of having just enough. We live in the sign of our present."
>—John Ashbery

"The poetic imagination does not resemble the eye, which can be put out for its offense, so much as it resembles the blood, which must be strengthened by feeding."
>—Muriel Rukeyser, *The Life of Poetry*

"For lack of everything, I imagine anything."
>—Keith Waldrop

Second from the bottom, in the gallery of generated faces, count fingers.

White solo cups: a giveaway.
Teeth like thumb tacks.
Urban Outfitters spaghetti straps, solids and stripes.
Nonexistent women going viral.

Observe the bold strokes of graphic. Digital cut-ups, if you wish.

The luxuriously coated pope has glasses melted into his blurred cheek, for instance.

Seventeen mylar castles, liquid in light. The nylon puffy jacket pavilions.

Here, indistinct astronauts huddle around the Eagle on the set.

The Getty watermark ghosting a double-A player
in grotesque sportsball.
The first digitally transparent deepfake.

Here above, a giraffe made of dragon and brontosaurus, circa sometime.
This strange could-scape was scanned from a human's brain.

Photographs overlain of two-to-four humans on a couch.
A mad libs parade of image-text-image lyric.

Or, two to four humans on a couch: an image-text-image mad lips.

A Lisa Frank Mona Lisa Mary.

Thumb, an impressionistic pharaoh.
Thumb, a photorealist angel of death.
Thumb, a Shepard Fairey filter.

Behold this neural mural selfie endgadget.

Bokeh light shining into the experiment.

A touch climbing alongside a how-to-draw cheek.

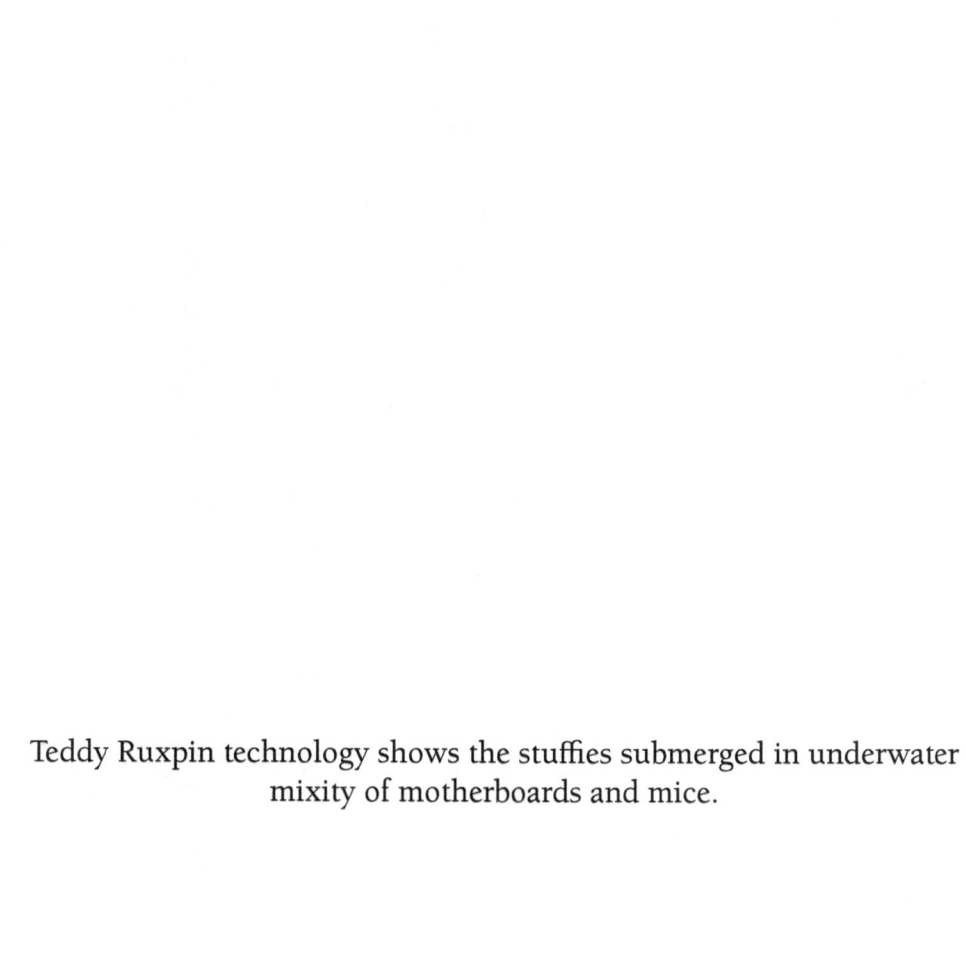

Teddy Ruxpin technology shows the stuffies submerged in underwater mixity of motherboards and mice.

Thumb faced guards sip tea from egg shaped cups at the coronation.

In other words,
welcome to Pose Estimation open prose.

Unlock your style. Generate.

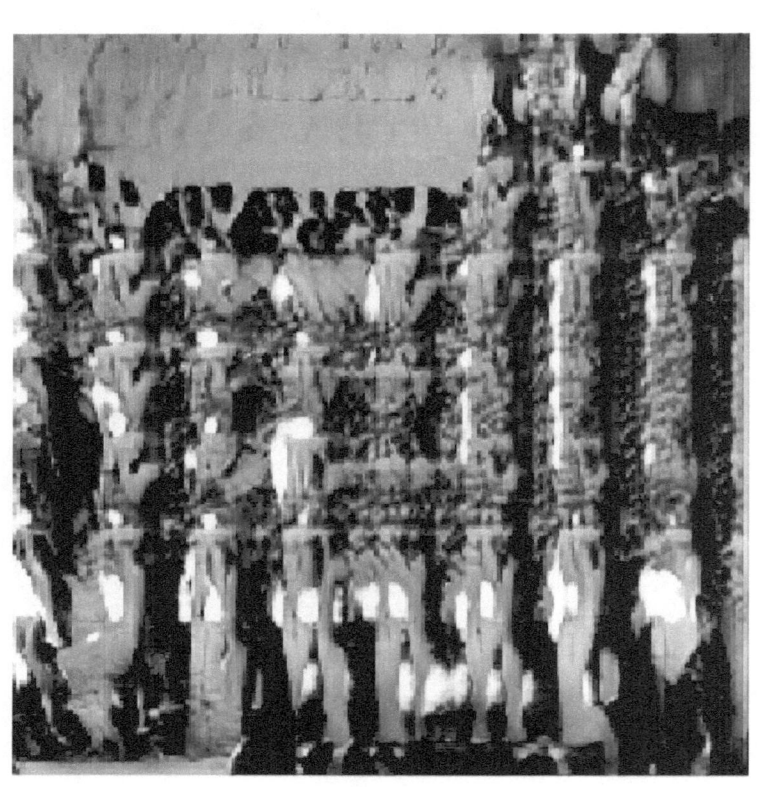

I photography news

I photography beautifier

I photography winner

I photography blender

I photography detector

i photography body

i photography editing

Ai Wei Wei photography

"Fake deep porn" yields authentic portraits of fill-in-the-blank thought.

Robo meat puppets sitting at attention behind desks that hide their genitals, looking dead center.

"Enter a caption mirror" yields a storefront.

"Plants planet blood weed" says the sign.

How violent to view the
Ultravioletto art
in *Endgadget* magazine.

In the background, foggy lettering, six bent fingers.

Hallucinatory artifact pressed urgently into a future hand rhizome.

Soldered knuckles of flesh capitalism shaped in arm-war prayer.

Beware the snipped feather mustache dusting the nation.

Consider the neural network of shopping cart cages.

"language hug" yields ad for Snuggie body bag.

Implied images of present surroundings suggest possibilities either above or around the corpse I.

w   do you   follow   ?

w   do you   search for ?

w   do you   go

w   you   die   ?

w   are you   still this

y   ?

AI inside human baskets of self checkouts.

I, not of platitudinal rain
but looky eye catching fall

not my mechanical I, searching
with an occasional tool

not solitude exactly
but something like it

outside the I space

the company one keeps exactly like them

paper I, with folded tabs and metal brads

fertile I, blooming
a thousand shapes of us es

I, like a bone
connecting
you to then and
then to marrow

I, ending
all-in like an
angry alarm clock

the shape of I inside the *it* inside itself
all personlike and leaning

it is tempting to see intelligent I's
in everything when they are not

apophenIA, I am reminded

I feel quite such really
all the time about everything

I just can't anymore

exquisite cicada I, not of song
of myself but beyond

I read "ferns, mosses, flags"
as "ferns" "mosses" "flags" and they all destroy me

a prism, says my daughter talking about her phone

I of suicidal light
what does it look like
under a ringtone

I, a comma
inserted numerically
into an empty space
between capitalist gory holes

I was alive and then I wasn't

comma one comma zero
It's not right that I'm alive

I watched incoming pixelated clouds
glitchy patches of grass plus
presidents teeing off

to vanishing points
of the two dimensional

to feel completely bedridden
with a belief of time
mossing itself all over the rock

I found inside grief

more grief
a hyperbolic curve
a parabolic you
I recognized a
bucolic opposite to
the empire of roman numerals

I heard a carbon monoxide alarm
screaming which dictionary
acronyms polite murder
a suicidal spoon
gouging grapefruit in public

I felt tipped

I rang the wrong number

I wanted to get out of bed sometimes

I thought
rounding out
all my senses into
an uncanny Q

I stopped asking

I, of the IV stretching
in red cursive across the
hospital screams

Into the bone of I, a femur for future anatomies of pronouns.

Many thanks to the journals in which excerpts of this poem first appeared, including *128 Lit*, and *Spirit Duplicator*.

Notes

p. 2, Inspired by AI photograph created by @mileszim and posted on Twitter. Reported by the *New York Post* on Jan. 16, 2023. https://nypost.com/2023/01/16/ai-generated-party-pics-look-eerily-real-unless-you-can-spot-these-tells/

p. 4, Inspired by *New York Times* article "Why Pope Francis is the Star of AI Photographs" published on April 4, 2023. https://www.nytimes.com/2023/04/08/technology/ai-photos-pope-francis.html

p. 5, Inspired by AI photograph that went viral and was created by @darylanselmo using MidJourney software on April 13, 2023. https://www.instagram.com/p/Cq-m8AyL5Qb/?igsh=MTc2cnQ3MzFpNDI5N-Q%3D%3D

p. 6, See *Guardian* article "The greatest photos ever? Why the moon landing shots are artistic masterpieces" by John Jones on July 17, 2019. https://www.theguardian.com/artanddesign/2019/jul/17/greatest-photos-ever-moon-landing-shots-artistic-masterpieces. See also "Astonishing AI restoration brings Apollo moon landing films up to speed" by Mindy Weisberger on Oct. 6, 2020. https://www.space.com/moon-landing-footage-remastered.html

p. 8,9,10, Inspired by Karen Hao's article "These weird, unsettling photos show that AI is getting smarter" in MIT Technology Review on Sept. 5, 2020: https://www.technologyreview.com/2020/09/25/1008921/ai-allen-institute-generates-images-from-captions/

p. 16: Based on photograph from Wikipedia article: "Teddy bears working on new AI research underwater with 1990s technology": https://en.m.wikipedia.org/wiki/File:CRAIYON-Teddy_bears_working_on_new_AI_research_underwater_with_1990s_technology.jpg

p. 19: "'Pose Estimation' is a computer vision task where the goal is to detect the position and orientation of a person or an object. Usually, this is done by predicting the location of specific key points like hands, head, elbows, etc. in case of Human Pose Estimation," according to Papers with Code, which describe it as "a free and open resource with Machine Learning papers, code, datasets, methods and evaluation tables." https://paperswithcode.com/task/pose-estimation and /about.

p. 20: AI photographs with the captions, in order: "A giraffe standing on dirt ground near a tree," "A woman attempting to ski on a flat hill," and "A zebra walking on a road with two cars approaching" generated by researchers at the Allen Institute for Artificial Intelligence (AI2) using a machine learning algorithm (X-LXMERT) that can produce images using only text captions as its guide. https://petapixel.com/2020/09/30/this-ai-generates-photos-using-only-text-captions/

p. 27: To be precise, *Endgadget* is an online tech blog owned by Yahoo. https://www.engadget.com/ Ultravioletto is an AI software that "explores the possibilities that lie between analog and digital fields to examine the relationship of humans and technology." https://ultraviolet.to/

p. 44: See, Martin Buber, "I and Thou."

p. 45: I was reminded specifically by Elle Longpre who wrote "apophenIa / apophenAIa" in light pencil of the margin of this manuscript, which was originally typewritten on a Royal: a choice born out of a necessity to remove myself from digital technology, specifically a Mac-Book, in order to observe it.

p. 48: First printed as a limited edition chapbook (A Soon Production ((soonproduction.org no longer found))) along with Peter Gizzi at "State of the Art" in Ithaca, NY on March 12, 2005. See Cordite Review, January 26, 2008 "Ferns, Mosses, Flags" by Elizabeth Willis.

p.57: "The Gender Panopticon: AI, Gender, and Design Justice" by Sonia K. Katyal and Jessica Y. Young. The Dukeminier Awards Journal, a journal out of the UCLA Williams Institute, 2002. Read: https://williamsinstitute.law.ucla.edu/wp-content/uploads/07-DAJ21-Katyal-Jung.pdf.

> In a world of more and more gender diversity, why is technology so committed to classification altogether? We propose it is not solely because of a conscious desire to exclude or to discriminate, but rather it is the consequence of inadequate design in a gender diverse population. But the cause of gender panopticism—and its effects—carry insights for anyone interested in the relationship between surveillance and gender. Since AI-driven technologies are largely committed to a fixed, binary framing of gender (and generally fail to grapple with its declining relevance in a gender diverse world), these technologies impose these frameworks onto populations that do not fit these categories, thereby reinscribing gender categories rather than challenging them. (p. 205, The Dukeminier Awards Journal)

A group of photographers

Acknowledgments

Thank you to the reader volunteers of Spuyten Duyvil but especially t thilleman and Aurelia.

Thank you to the editors of *128 Lit* and *Spirit Duplicator* in which parts of this poem have first appeared.

Thank you to everyone who read early versions of this manuscript including Adam Tobin, Elle Longpre, Ry Cook, Patrick Milian, and Zoe Tuck.

Thank you to everyone I've worked with at Wave Books, but especially Douglas Kearney, Dara Barrois-Dixon, CAConrad, Dorothea Lasky, Don Mee Choi, Geoffrey Nutter, Heidi Broadhead, and Joshua Beckman. Thank you always, Peter Gizzi.

To my loves, my sister Margaret and my mom Judy: thank you for always supporting my writing. Thank you to my stepfamilies, including my stepmom Missey and my stepdad Gerard.

For my loves, Ursula and Adam: I write for you.

In memory of my dad, Jack D.

CATHERINE BRESNER is the author of the chapbooks *The Merriam Webster Series* (2012); *Some Break A / Others Say Do* (forthcoming 2024, Press Brake); the artist book *Everyday Eros* (Mount Analogue 2017); and the poetry collection *the empty season*, which won the Diode Edition Book Prize in 2017. Her poetry has appeared or is forthcoming in *FENCE*, the *VOLT*, *b l u s h*, *Denver Quarterly*, *Sixth Finch*, *Fonograf*, *Iterant*, *The Offing*, *Paperbag* and elsewhere. Currently, she is the publicist for Wave Books and co-edits *Spirit Duplicator*, a biannual mimeograph magazine of poetry and art, with the poet Adam Tobin. She believes in a free Palestine.